PALACE OF MEMORY: AN ELEGY

By the same author

Books
Moonlight on Oleander (2018)
Ikaros (2017)
Gallery of Antique Art (2016)
Burnt Umber (2016)
Watching the World: Impressions of Canberra (2015) (with Jen Webb)
Six Different Windows (2013)
It Feels Like Disbelief (2007)
Blood and Old Belief: A Verse Novel (2003)
Stepping Away: Selected Poems (2001)
Canvas Light (1998)
Shadow Swimmer (1995)
The Dancing Scorpion (1993)
Acts Themselves Trivial (1991)

Chapbooks
Wedding Dress and Other Poems (2018)
Prosody: Enjambment (2018)
Colours: Blue (2017)
The Taoist Elements: Earth (2016)
Jars (2015)
Viscera (2014)
Chicken and Other Poems (2012)
Mapping Wildwood Road (1990)

PALACE OF MEMORY: AN ELEGY

PAUL HETHERINGTON

RECENT
WORK
PRESS

Palace of Memory: An elegy
Recent Work Press
Canberra, Australia

Copyright © Paul Hetherington, 2019

ISBN: 9780648404255 (paperback)

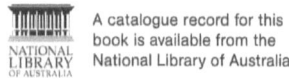
A catalogue record for this book is available from the National Library of Australia

All rights reserved. This book is copyright. Except for private study, research, criticism or reviews as permitted under the Copyright Act, no part of this book may be reproduced, stored in a retrieval system, or transmitted in any form by any means without prior written permission. Enquiries should be addressed to the publisher.

Cover image: IMG_7056 by Raquel Baranow reproduced under Creative Commons Attribution-ShareAlike 2.0 Generic licence
Cover design: Recent Work Press
Set by Recent Work Press

recentworkpress.com

for Michelle

1.

Worn stones support façades with the cold press of forgetfulness—so much moss and lichen-covered ruin. What has been known is trickling water; slippery rock; the searching finger. What belongs is broken, like a Catholic palace after the Reformation.

//

Sky peers down with the gaze of a forgetful god—'too late' cry undressed stones. There's an old structure; a form of belief no longer whole. Words from the pulpit resonate in the northern breeze, blown into incoherence. The old order lurches within the body's fret and bone.

2.

After all, it isn't entirely ruined, sprawling on the hillside, rain rolling on the nearby orchard like a wrestler. Columns support gaggles of stone. A tangled drive turns. The portico's doors are an insect's eye. A long view opens a passageway; a cavity burns with yellow.
//
Across the threshold a pendulum shudders in a large house-clock; a shadow stands in a doorway. *He stood like Hamlet's ghost, motionless and speechless.* Voices speak loudly from another room. A long-nosed man winds the mechanism.

3.

A dim way. Tall, curtained windows rising, like my father. Every shadow's an adhesive stain. My footsteps sound—someone is walking behind the wall. In the first large room, a tumbleweed of light falls and runs. Candelabras, upholstered chairs, waterfalls of tapestries. They solidify into dogs, a fox, a hunter with a horse. Another's a battle scene where blood hangs in a hundred woven petals. A table with sepia eyes stares back.

4.

There's a gallery where the voices of paintings are loud. Colours and daubs confuse—like mixed expletives; like riding a sled through burning snow. I look for quiet in a storeroom among spear guns, nylon ropes, wetsuits.

//

Waves suck; I try to grab the wide green. A buoy bounces and rears, my mind's an orange slash and red smear. I pull arms forward, throwing them down.

//

I'm a painting of a child, abstracted, lost in the seethe. The colours are saying 'your flesh is ours, your body is broken, you have no wings'. Sand meets my stretched toes.

5.

I imagined my father may once have been a Turkish merchant but, if so, he'd given the business away. As I grew up, I thought him regular in his approach to everything. He made it a rule to wind his watch every morning, sitting at the breakfast table with upright pieces of toast and the butter and jam he'd liberally spread on them. *We were so used to minutes, hours, weeks, and months.*

//

As bombs fell in an extended line, they marked the plane's direction before it banked. My father saw them stepping towards him as a vigorous row of exclamation marks—but with the monotonous emphasis of a rhetorician who knows only repetition.

//

In his later life, my father buttered his toast generously, as if to remember the occasion, when he was spread out flat on the earth's dark rye.

6.

Looking at shattered walls, wanting my sense of fracture to heal. I've garnered loss weighing like furniture. Gestures I carry are heavier still. Lovers are sculptures in the park, pressing hands to one another's bodies, as if chiselling feeling.

//

There are passages of stone relief. Foundations leak, discarded items are spilled in hallways. A man rises from a bed in yellow light. He's impossibly stretched, taller than the ceiling (his head rests against it). Like a worn-out god, flesh a tatter on his chalky bones, he explains my insufficiencies.

7.

Corridors lead to servants' quarters. I stray towards a wide fire and a clash of knives, ducking into a side room where a man chewing tobacco plays backgammon against himself. I'm soon at the table and he becomes calmer, guiding my hand. But he's a shadow; his hand's pressure disappears from my arm. The backgammon pieces spill. I'm part of a threadbare tapestry.

8.

People are burning the past. Documents fly and fall, so that I begin to read the lawn. Accounts and memos declare who's obliged—but the grass and fire don't know this. We tread on passages as the fire flares; words fall as ash. We read ourselves in the marks—misconstrued, wanting a salve. Why don't we destroy what we burn?

9.

A train gathers glint-metres of time. Twenty-years-old we drag doors and jump on; your shopping bag trails a scarf; the closing door holds. As we wrestle the handle, the scarf flags above a reaching five-year-old (that's me, too, watching carriages slide on summer's shine). A young woman stands as green fabric eludes her hand. I open a bag; sky bleeds from brown paper.

10.

We hurry past fences, seeing the red sky. *The rubies about thy neck are flying over our heads like light clouds of a windy day.* There are rotting factories and a distant engine churning noise like a remorseless dream. You gather a scrap of newspaper with a headline reading, 'They Have Now Embarked'.

//

We stumble onto a portico where doors crowd; where a low fire burns with distempered yellow. We enter, looking at the gleaming furniture and a 78 circling an ancient turntable: Beethoven's ninth symphony. My father's hands grasp the disc. He's forty-two.

11.

After the ambulance departs we stand outside the closed cafe and talk about summer plans—'perhaps a cottage on a mountain; maybe a chalet on a beach?' We go separate ways. Days later you read about a dead physician, who left behind four young children and a wife. 'It couldn't have been him,' you say. We both imagine the face of the fallen man, staring with a vagrant smile. Shuddering, you push your leg against mine.

12.

I step fingers on your spine,
each one a stone in a creek, or a stilt-walker balancing on a
strung wire.

13.

The library has a thousand books. I open an old volume where fluent notions spill like rain. Then there's a collection of wrinkled, discoloured leaves in my hand—I think of the way they purpled and faded; how lost sunsets shine like ideas.
//
Leaves fall from gaps in the cornices; the library becomes a wintry forest; the radio announces a national emergency. I watch the clock's ratcheting hands.

14.

In the bathroom my father glances at me over his electric razor. He's thirty-six, the year after I was born, and my mother sings in another room. He turns to the mirror and I see that his hands are bars of shadow, his face an impression of sunlight, his towel-wrapped body a feint in the air. When I squalled in a cot he was hardly real—except for his grasp, the smell of his breath.

15.

A bath floats with wax sculptures, their surfaces blackened by mould. I brush my teeth and they roll in water that looks like mercury. Later, catching the edges of dreams, they march as soldiers or congregate like intimates (if it's not them, who has turned the pillow?). They loll for hours in sunshine and will not move—wantons; or characters in a *fin de siècle* novel.

16.

We might be light that silently climbs the columns. We hear gulls calling and the insouciance of winds, riding the hills' topography where green touches our thought. We lift on thermals. We become more like words, more and more an entwining of complex grammar, as you ask me to speak for you—and the sentence drifts, expressing solitude, carrying me towards isolation that stands as a statue in memory. Are these your breeze-like words wrapping my face and are your arms lengthening like sunshine?

17.

A line about fabulation turns in my head—a sense of the exquisite. Is it the borrowing of touch from another, a gesture like the fragrance of lime, or the glorious open-handedness of sunflowers in bloom, a darkness at their frothing centre? I live between existences, and this skyline might be any city. I'm wafted on memory; sometimes in anticipation of beauty. There's no way to account for my perambulations; streets make new patterns on my soles. If there's a way of inhabiting the mysterious, this day might be the vehicle. A child speaks in my voice, conjuring old forms of longing. I'm once again picking a yellow flower and holding it against the sun.

18.

There is no plank in reason. Ideas tumble. Feelings are pressing forwards and will fall.

//

'I' is a pronoun spoken in a play. A ghost in an orchard where woodcutters sharpen axes. A man on battlements who lives in childhood.

//

He mouths woe, wandering about the windy stone. Why was his leaving so untimely? What was the name he gave me?

//

What I remember cannot be my name. I search for it in paragraphs of water; in deceitful shines of rain.

19.

The cityscape stretches from my gaze so that plazas and squares are elongated, complex equations. Statues twist and stoop; uneasiness fills the blowing air as if the Fall still resonates; as if words are tainted. A fox runs across cobblestones, and soldiers follow. A voice wonders, 'have we outlived the twentieth century?' Two girls skip with a rope, and a third joins them. The first two stretch the rope so she can jump as they turn. Her legs are caught.

20.

The palace has shrunk to three rooms. There's my mother at ninety; here she is at nine. She sits on a stool and milks a cow. Flies hover and sing. The palace steps backwards, expanding until its rooms recede for a year, as unreachable as Banquo's children.

//

We are five years old, walking towards the sound of voices. The next room must hold them. The room after the next. The room beyond the corridor. The side porch. Even the driveway is empty.

//

We turn, because the voices are behind us. Two girls kiss in the bathroom with handfuls of hair. A string of saliva is a sagging tightrope. The kitchen is hung with silver pans. We walk towards a burning fire. You find a folded letter beneath the grate, and the voices are upon us. You stuff it into your pocket.

21.

She leans on a spade in the garden, sizing up peas and tomatoes. Inside the hallway she speaks of 'fencing' and 'what we might do'. On a blue sofa he eats an Anzac biscuit, as she conjures a man 'who was killed'. Even at nine years old, in these 1960s suburbs he senses the proximity of the war. A marching song, traipse of boots, a comment about how the garden would have known him. A grey picture with a fixed, elusive glance. Cropped hair, a sense of insouciance. At eighteen, a farmer's son. Uncaptured steps he took beyond the scene.

22.

I am constituted in the sketching motion of hands. Until my thought ends; until the fountain in this garden stops spilling water onto the lawn. She always stoops and says: 'What an absurd day, because you remind me ... turn your face upwards'; and, 'Yes, yes ...' Her hands at my throat, her sudden, recoiling awareness, a shakingly-proffered cup. In the one photograph, his dark eyes—liquid sight flowing over the house and lawn.

23.

Between stations, she's among flowers, pressing herself against light, picking colours of memory in red and yellow heads.

//

There's a stairway turning down eight flights, a man talking quickly. She remembers her body arching, the sensation of teetering, words pushing her backwards.

//

She closes her journal on the flowers, thinking of the expedition ahead. Light falls like a stairway from low clouds, but she cannot climb.

24.

Night falls and stars weigh. Figures that might be down-at-heel angels are in the garden and my father's hand is on my head. 'Come on boy,' he says, trailing a cricket bat in his right hand, bouncing a ball. He climbs a tall tree and stares down like Fagus, stroking his beard.

//

He dives into a running ocean and beckons as he swims, alight with phosphorescence. If I were to touch him he'd burn like a torch.

//

I see he's saying something important but I can barely hear him. I lean closer as the words dissolve, and everything's out-of-date. Night's constellations hang like an absurd, intricate chandelier as he states he has to leave—even as a tall tree demurs. I try to speak but my words are someone else's: 'you must know, your father lost a father'.

25.

My father's breathing is a gasp; hospital sheets are awkwardly pulled and tucked; forgettable words begin to overwrite him.

//

Before an affliction is digested consolation ever comes too soon; and after it is digested, it comes too late: so that there is but a mark between these two, as fine almost as a hair, for a comforter to take aim at.

//

Dates vanish, the dead are laid down. There's a still tree in a front yard, a scribble of chalk on a board, a squirming sea. He swims out and away. I walk on a white road; stumble from a tall swing. I'm at a zoo, eating ice cream in a cone that melts as I stand. A tap fills a bucket, that he lifts. He carries a child with a broken arm, his breath is fragrant smoke.

26.

Memory says we were never together there—climbing wide slopes, tasting exertion in our mouths. Wind brushes dunes like a hand worrying a coat. You look towards the ocean and see a life ploughing through waves, like a father you'd never known sailing back from war's hideous theatre—his uniform cold with medals and starch. Making art wouldn't quell your misgivings; you ran the dune-line, punishing yourself. Love never answered in the way you wanted.

27.

Columns, hallways, the room where they'd waited. Yellow, distracted light; words that said 'leave' or 'come', the sound of their footsteps on paving stones. A man sits near a cake stand. The man nods, holding a cupcake that smells of caramel. If he were to bite, seeing crumbs fall. 'I don't remember.' But what does the phrase mean now, when memory is within us like corpuscles? Where we've been, there are shreds and ashes of time— in that garden, where she points and leans. The spreading flower, the shrub tugged from its ground. The 44-gallon drum smoking. 'I have no way of making good.'

28.

The old building peers like a beginning or end. It's more than eighty years since she lived there. Corrugations trap light; paddocks and scrub run into distance. Her brothers shove each other as she sits, milking patiently. The cow shifts its feet; she stretches her hand; milk glistens. She sees undulations of light, her father hauling a chain, the tractor's dirty smoke. There's liquid on the rim of a 44-gallon drum. 'Lie still.'

//

The bedsheets wrap her like a pressing body. She turns, faces the wall. Belief is a fracture of birds, their cries splitting in air. A hawk, a bloodied feather. Knowledge is dry air and quick words.

29.

We are in front of the blue sea—a post-Impressionist painting of two young women. One rows; one holds a parasol, ripples invoke sky and breeze. One says to the other 'will you love me?' The other has an expression like water. They look towards the shore, and inwards into history. You say, 'I cannot answer' as if to the distant white cliff; as if to one of the women. I'm holding your hand; the ocean is an opaque slate-green.

30.

'So, I've decided to write this. It's been hard to admit how ruined I feel. If I were a building you'd find me in Venice's poorest quarter, next to murky water. You tell me you've no obligation, yet it's unimaginably hard, quelling these feelings. Now, I'm like the gargoyle on our favourite church, looking into the reflection of my changed face. Can you remember our enthusiasm?'

31.

He walked across the yard, clanging the gate. The old moon weighed like a boulder. As much as he tried, he couldn't catch her; he was unable to decipher her words. He saw himself talking to her, pointing the way, arm in arm, as the brown and roiling river danced with ideas of the future. He saw her climb away on a thin beam of light.

32.

Years tumbled through the sky like grainy efflorescence, and his dear friend stood in front of the view, spreading wings. Six years dead, yet he spoke of recent things—of art he'd made, of writing he'd composed. The sky showed indecipherable inscriptions, as if from a sacred book. Galaxies turned, his friend took ungainly flight, like an ancient bird pushing into wind.

33.

'In Darwin in 1942 I was last out of the mess hut, I don't remember why ... I didn't have time to reach the slit trench.' *A man of deep reading—prompt memory.* 'I saw the Japanese bombs falling in a line towards me and thought I was dead. I followed my training, dropping to the ground, holding my helmet with both hands. One bomb fell in front of me and one fell behind, dirt from the explosions raining.' *As with the advantage of a death's-head before him.*

//

Dozing in the mess hut, thinking the sirens were another drill. Dreaming of going to school, entering a classroom. The teacher is Death, dressed in bones, saying, 'Scrub your name from the blackboard'. *Even for an eggshell.*

//

'Perhaps I was reading ....' *If any such reading as this could be supposed to hold out so long— to the very end of the world.*

34.

  His mother is a schoolgirl running along a path next to paddocks, her brother following. That morning a girl had hung herself with a cord from a rafter, her lunchbox at her feet, an essay neatly written in her bag. Her note says, 'I'm full with shame.'
  //
  A woman says, 'The taxi's waiting', but the city's a clot of memories that won't be mapped or traversed. The skyline glares and smog blurs the sunset. That old rural world ghosts it like a palimpsest—implacable drought and a one-room school.
  //
  'I couldn't believe she would do that.'

35.

The words of childhood are heavy and strong. 'Come here.' 'Behave.' 'Don't you dare.' So many cling to thought like stones, or splash in a creek over a folded rock. Water bubbles and curls towards a light-bristling pool. A girl shouts, hoisting her bathers; a boy spits water like a sermon in church; a woman idles like a languorous verb. Language weighs as we try to stand. Words in the car are like wasps in the ear.

36.

After thirty years you knocked on my door: 'Why didn't we follow the quilted sunset?' Your words spiral in formal inflections. You tell a story about thwarted hopes that carry decades on their backs. I would disencumber you of history and memory. I'd show you kind letters, and take us back to mutuality.

37.

In a river's slip-clack of pebbles, an ocean's folding-rooms of waves; within a worn door's skied keyhole, a fountain's half-hoops of rainbow; in a stranger's gait that trips on our past, your hands on a windowsill flexing like squids, a wide field where grass addresses your feet. Your hands kept it too, there, by the sea, lost from our cities. And words we agreed on by not speaking out.

38.

We are shadows thrown on walls and doors, our future a collection of window views. You point to domes and spires, blue patches of parkland. We turn and find a space we'd left years previously. You are intimate and unselfconscious in that room, in a far suburb, placing flowers in a vase, arranging them one by one, cutting stalks, making them into an artwork. 'I'll paint them,' you say, picking up brushes. We talk of this city—how one day we'll find a destination. You describe the paintwork and the stain on the wall you think you'll see: 'A place to belong.' It was a future that the past had relinquished—and, strangely, we were there.

39.

How they wander and halt: those ghosts in my house, and words on the floor. We tread on the past and slip—into old imprecations; old assertions and hatreds. Who brought them here and laid them down? Who pushed poison into our ears? My father walks through open spaces, as if searching for something. My mother remembers, lost in thought. Food jams a table, red wine is broached—but that meal was consumed. Words, like fingers, trail recollection—as if memory's a species of rejuvenated touch. *Pity me not. My hour is almost come.* I grasp my father but he's only air. *Lend thy serious hearing.* What crossed our horizons through misspeakings? What griefs do we deny?

40.

Although we loved abstruse thought, academic even to the laces of our shoes, our family was a machine consisting of a few wheels. Yet they were set in motion by many different springs acting upon each other with a variety of impulses and passions. Our machine had all the advantages of complexity, with many odd movements.

//

In the family, a remark was soon an extrapolating conversation or took the shape of a debate. And each occasion had its machine simplicities; though every instance brought subtle or brutal differences.

//

Further, whatever motion, harangue, dialogue or project was going forwards, there was often another proceeding at the same time ... *How finely we argued upon mistaken facts!*

41.

Pebbles full-stop the path. Where we'd walked, we are walking again. But this time your body's a wafting of air. This time the path opens towards hills we will not climb. You point, saying, 'so many umbers and blues. Do not forget.' I'd played the scene previously, when you were ill, under thought's proscenium. I stood in the idea we had of each other and knew it wouldn't be complete. Many unrehearsed speeches.

42.

Where the hallway turns, you find a nineteenth-century letter. Its paper crumbles; a nurse's account of the Burmese war. We can't stomach the cruelty. The British Raj crosses the border; resisters' villages and possessions are burned; a culture is melted. We were going to rent the house, settle, find a way forward. Instead, we make for the front door, ducking under a laden almond tree.

//

As a child, I played under a heavy tree, shooting the incorrigible enemy. Almonds were boyhood's shrapnel.

//

The letter has bodies heaped in mounds. Our inheritance begins to press. Gesturing at tall houses, you flail.

43.

We touched what neither of us had previously encountered, and could never speak of it in the past tense. In a room where space opened like a hub of light. Shadows hesitated and shifted, as in a puppet show. Time moves us as if we don't belong within it; space is an idea we improvise, without dimensions. You open conversations on a thousand subjects but finish none. It's not that we have too little to say, but that we're continually being brought to new considerations—affection fiercely persists while nothing between us ever knows its age.

44.

A tree stands in the middle of a large room. Days are held there too, which people walk through—yet, close as they are, we can't converse. Weeks are stilled there, like something in aspic. Years peer down chimneys, studying their obsolescence. My father climbs the tree, moving from branch to branch. A girl lies in a creek, saying she is watchman to my heart. But who speaks in such ways? The present moment is tangled with time, pulling and knotting thought. An owl swerves. The baker's daughter dusts flour from her hands.

45.

The room was liquid, like a glass of swirled whisky. You were a shadow on walls; a fugitive shifting of light and space between a shutter's cast and a blue tablecloth. That's where we met—between day and night's radiance. An apple in the hand, umbrageous feeling; thought as a place of waiting. We were drowned for days, without narratives to dress us, sifting memory through hands. Was it an old sense of being? A school of small fish? A tide to swallow the room.

46.

'To be safe was to be stranded from identity. I saw a shoreline and tower; I saw women in a ring. They were distant; I would never be among them. I looked across the ocean and saw no horizon. I stood in a small room. My face became another's face, lids stiffening; eyes glazed. More and more I was Galatea being made from an ordinary woman. Increasingly I felt my breath as if it blew a studio's dust; remembered his hands all over my body.'

//

'Safety—to meander nowhere, and never know the streets. To call myself by a name that my skin doesn't know, narrate another's life as my own, disavow intimate being. If I were skinned alive I'd be more self than this—now unable to touch his separateness; feeling his being like something I might wear on my chest, panting. Where is that part I left in his mouth?'

47.

Beside the cricket pitch a broken watch ticks on the early season's grass. He runs in to bowl and the red ball swings. The batsman hits hard ... a train winds up a hill. He looks from a window to see a boy hurl the ball and the batsman sprinting towards his crease: one run to win. The umpire raises his finger as fielders appeal ... a hawk hovers over hedgerowed countryside. Now he's looking at a man who turns out of an avenue, walking towards a mausoleum. He knows the gait, calls out the boy's name. When he reaches the mausoleum, no-one's there. The ball is tight in his hand; time's alleys are closing.

48.

The black-painted fence at Hanwell Station is a mass of seated, congregated spears. West Ealing arrives soon enough and London's skies flex. A protracted summer reaches into autumn; we think of Keats in love with poetry. You liked the late Romantics, and ideas of connection to salve solitude, *drinking water from the chained cup*, enthusing over high-flung speech. Today I'd clasp your book and remember companionable talk, look away from angry politics. I'd remember the quench of speaking.

49.

We saw ourselves inhabiting unfamiliar spaces—as if a nineteenth-century mirror's old shapes and destinations clambered over us. A tall woman in dark Victorian dress was instructing maids, her accents so gentle she might have been humming. A parrot sat on a windowsill and whistled an American Civil War marching tune. The washed faces of boys lay on the glass with a mercury shine. They were pushing hair into place, looking towards a future that would leave them as bones. We saw a man on stilts stealing a cloth bag from a child. 'I'll chase him down,' you said, 'and throw him over.' But the mirror had moved.

50.

One foot after another, turning into and climbing the tower. After three landings and four hundred and twenty-three steps I escape into cold air, night and mist. He's standing with a hat on his head and won't speak. My hand on his chest finds no purchase. It's as if my fingers push through his heart—as if, reaching, I grab handfuls of our mutual past. Gobbets of it slide between fingers. He is unmoved, miming a speech that never leaves his mouth. I wish to memorialise him but he won't answer questions—there is so much I never asked while he was alive. He's finding his antic disposition. Gaps in the floor open; he skips across them. He falls.

51.

We are standing in the swirling tail of the storm. Trees whip and slash, the world out of sorts. Time runs against our bodies, like sand on the wind. I see a cup thrown in a room and bend to pick up the pieces. 'A newer Sevres pleases,' her voice says, and despite our argument we smile. 'Happy birthday,' she says, hauling a present from the cupboard. She was nineteen, inhabited by a sense of being bruised. 'I remember her,' you say. I remember her hands wanting a decision. We touched each other as if we were making an unreal life solid. Like porcelain, those kisses had the flavour of the world's end.

52.

Gates and alleys of the mind are open. In this dusk silence holds the moon as if it's a chunk of something broken—it might be love, with its weedy laneways. One wind-boisterous day we looked for wild plants and found words beneath the soil—or crouching under leaning struts of mushrooms.

//

I can't find them now; they sung in ways that addressed our lack and loss. Today, my father walks across the bricks he long since laid, as if another time creeps through the brown-hued air, and his utterance precedes him—an old and well-told joke from his time at war, dying at the sight of falling bombs. The moon's ray is a renaissance sword and his second afterlife runs me through.

53.

Dark light, a thrashing of words. If it's memory, it's also a slash of foliage against the eyes, a broken pane, the intrusion of another's thought like the scrambling flurry of a nesting bird. We walked against tight gusts of air, my mother and father leading, gathering distance. We saw wide thrusts of the sea and later circled rock pools that showed striations of green on rocks that cut the feet. Something was amiss. It began to rain, the bird flew past, the sky and sea in querulous argument.

54.

Small things grip us—damaged cutlery, an album of photographs we're throwing away. We remember an oak leaning into black shade. Your words hold, speaking of cities you've visited—Rome, Berlin, London—and the towns where you grew up, surrounded by wide country. The farm machinery shop was one of your father's favourite places, away from crops and the kitchen. You speak of it as if an angel was letting down her wings on that past; as if there were too many feelings you'd never recover. 'The oak reminds me,' you say, speaking of incandescent summers and a horse you rode. The album shows a man standing on the bonnet of a large tractor, dwarfed by a fierce sky—he might have been declaiming his lordship of the land. 'An odd intimacy?' you said, 'Wind blew dust for days.'

55.

She was standing in a tapestry in a distant room. He had ducked past ropes and 'do not enter' signs. The ancient palace was mostly off limits now, except for the new gallery and public courtyard. This tapestry was from fourteenth-century Arras, its blues and reds still subtly cool and fiercely burning. She was holding herself apart from an affray. He recognised the anticipation in her body. He sensed a breeze—threads of her hair were blown back.

56.

Thought burns through the night. The old things are no longer old. Convictions are an explosion of light. Memory's palace flares.

57.

With imperfections on his head, he's studying battlements he once constructed—made of boughs and awkward sentences, stuffed tight with tearing purpose. At evening he eats his mother's arguments and meals, still charting moors and river-winding country. His queen is with him, carrying the white-flowered burden of being kind. A teacher advises a middle path; his dark-haired father talks of what is right. But poetry's the border's fascination. The pithy, unmannered word.

58.

As I fall, *sotto voce,* towards old prospects of mind, I'm a sail on winds of past intemperance. I become wind itself, gliding past a mainsail; become a large idea hung across a breeze. A hand swipes across time as if it's a screen, a girl giggles, a man on a beach gasps. You hold him towards his life as his face pales. You prop him back into time, and he staggers away. The girl is behind a dune where wind has quietened. She speaks of stars, pushing a needle into her arm. You wonder what you rescued. Time is the blanket weighing heavily on your chest.

59.

Night air is cold, his hand's upon my shoulder pointing—a gesture indicating glossy futures. He points far ahead and indicates what's close, as if distance might collect this day and minute. The gestures do not settle, bumping about the brain. It's like an unused phrase—neglected because the occasion vanished. He stands in mind and eye as a homunculus, bedraggled in rain or staring at the sun. He speaks of the impossible as true, like an orator on a shrink-wrapped stage. Once his canny dreams were a rising ovoid.

60.

We finish a bottle of wine and open another. It's better, and we fill our glasses. The year teeters; we are suddenly looking forwards, even as we examine artefacts from the past. You read a poem by Sappho about her brothers, say 'As the sweet apple grows red on the topmost branch', and we consider what is precious and neglected. The year might be swerving into dissolution, but we look away, enjoying our convivial noise. Another poet's lines are raised on high, as if there might be laurel in the room. You whisper, 'what have we forgotten?'

61.

I recognised myself as a child in a department store, trying to grasp a box of chocolates. They looked larger than a washing machine. I heard a woman say 'let's mend the seams', and heard another, laughing: 'I know not seams.' I was image and wild idea, barely human. I pushed at my stomach, feeling where they'd opened and stitched my skin. The ache was mortality. A woman in water was a slivered glimpse, stopping time. Generations back, my mother's father's mother. He was failing to revive her again.

62.

We clasp him to us like a package of light—the child who ran towards the reeds. But our hands are flexing, our thoughts are travelling away. We open arms and the world rushes in. A line of cars leaves the picnic ground; coats and scarves are left on yellowed grass. We look at water floating with debris, reflecting the canopy of elm and oak. We see the creek's channel run towards a diminishing gleam. Where we stand, there have been too many footsteps.

63.

A girl runs out of a picture frame, missing half her body, her hair blown back in a strange, unruly curl. No-one's sure who she is—or who the photographer is—although she's also in two other snaps. She's dressed in red at a party, wearing a paper crown. She stands on a dune in front of a turbulent ocean. A blue-capped swimmer waves.

64.

We can't be certain we were ever there—in the city's piazza at night where a woman on stilts threw marshmallows and juggled fire. You grabbed my arm; spoke of your parents abandoning you. We drank martinis, the bartender eventually saying 'make your own and leave the money'. You confessed you loved a man who'd deserted you—'as if it's all pointless repetition'. Did we see the same woman running with the bulls? And in what city did you write me, 'Goodbye'? I eventually found you in a café with a friend of mine where you shrugged and refused to speak. He clasped me by the hand. Memory's cities: a false conclusion; a part to play that doesn't fit.

65.

It's my father telling me off in the back yard, asking me to give him the box of matches. It might be a still life. He faces me squarely. Night is heavy with stars, like thousands of glints in an estuary. I give him the box, holding the flame in mind—and he takes it even as the fire remains between us—being chastised, flexing burnt fingers.

66.

    The clock doesn't wind, though the ratchets seem to turn. The hands stay where they are, so many years ago. The mechanism is obdurate; years fall on the face like a dry waterfall.
    //
    Cascading with images, ticking through episodes. *If there are three drops of oil to be got, and a hammer to be found.*
    //
    I walk on a plank in memory and a creek runs under me. I hesitate, seeing the froth and curl of water. The branches that dam the flow are being overturned. My image dives.
    //
    A swell has hold of us; the tide's drag has hold. My uncle flails in the ocean, panting 'Can you get to shore?' My heart's a rapid metronome; my thoughts are torn. I nod 'yes', arm over arm, barely moving.

67.

He slits the envelope, knowing the handwriting. The letter's crisp blue paper nearly cuts his finger, even as a hint of perfume assails him—just as it had with her first invitation. He decides he won't read it, drinks a glass of Nocello. He drinks another glass and decides he'll glance at the looping words. Eleven years bracketed by identical paper; a sensation like a caterpillar on skin. A memory of her body hesitating at the periphery of feeling. 'Speechless,' she says—'which is to say, I can't indicate what I mean.' Children shout outside in their games, circling a scarecrow in a dry field. He sees her naked among the fine silks she'd dragged from storage, 'that my husband gave'. As if enmeshed in a hundred shades, saying 'quickly'.

68.

The small plane lurches, lifts on a cushion of air. He stifles his sense of illness, settles uncomfortably, and is cocooned in words, though nobody speaks; noisy engines burr. Extravagant things they said are magnified as he continually fails to understand. A hostess offers a snack, and the pilot apologises for the delay. He trawls thought for what he's believed, and for something beautiful in speech. There are sentences she wrote that seem all of intimacy.

69.

I'm not looking towards land, but towards the explorations of insouciant verbs. They've carried me far out. The day is unnameable; my solace is the memory of a girl straddling my chest. She is like a mouthful of sea; I hesitate at the perimeter of new expression, the dipping hemline of her dress.

70.

The laneway falls towards cottages. A boy enters a low doorway, time's wrinkles fold. A path falls away from a walking girl and wind blows her words sideways. She looks towards the future but the hill's rising slant traps her feet like a high tide. She can't easily walk out of there; feels history rising towards her knees; tries to push through it, looks to a boat that plies its way. The boy emerges and she sees a future in his gait. The laneway drags like a tied rope.

71.

Water drips, as if to clog time. Yet it runs fast about these stones on the wind; spreading the afternoon in flurries and squalls. The palace is deserted; its stones sound only with the feet of those who have left. So many long rooms stripped of all that made them hospitable.

//

Yet my mother and father are in the banqueting hall. They talk of meat they've bought, of wine they'll drink. I walk towards their voices—which have moulded and licked me, each like a bear with a cub.

//

I recollect the caress, turning the corner, but only my mother waits. She hardly hears my greeting, turning stiffly through old age as if partly stone. *My mother was going very gingerly in the dark.* Her words are clear, like an abraded skeleton of our past loquaciousness. My father stands like a ghost on a stage, mouthing sentences: *I have some rights of memory in this kingdom.*

//

Time's rivulets /

are flooding thought /

Afterword

The sequence of prose poems, *Palace of Memory: An elegy* explores the elusive and troubling territory of recollection, not only referring to and problematising the ancient idea of the art of memory (*ars memoriae*) but also traversing the way in which memory is unreliable or incomplete. In doing so, it highlights the close connection between personal memory and sensory experience, as well as the powerful role played by visual imagery in recollection.

Palace of Memory is as much about relics and the persistence of unfinished structures of the mind as about what is lost or forgotten. It focuses on an understanding of the father and mother and the way memory represents an evolving, tangled and sometimes paradoxical inheritance for every individual, as they fashion identity's self-narrations. The apparently firm ground of the present is revealed as vulnerable to intrusive aspects of the past; memory's tinder.

This prose poetry sequence may also be read as a succession of ghostings—spectral fragments that are continually being overwritten by other texts and diverse experiences. From this perspective, identity becomes a progression of palimpsests connected to a fractured memory-hoard that is ceaselessly reconstructed and rewritten even as parts of it are razed to the ground.

Acknowledgements

Palace of Memory: An elegy is to some extent an intertextual work. Its main intertexts are Laurence Sterne's *The Life and Opinions of Tristram Shandy, Gentleman* and William Shakespeare's *Hamlet*. As well as these two works, *Palace of Memory* uses or refers briefly to texts by Sappho (adapting a translation of a Sapphic line by Amanda Kubic); Emily Dickinson (particularly the poems 'I felt a Funeral, in my Brain,' and 'I stepped from Plank to Plank'); and Dylan Thomas ('The Hunchback in the Park'). Additionally, there are one or two other allusions. However, in order to avoid disrupting the flow of this prose poetry sequence, not all quotations from, allusions to, or paraphrases of sections of the texts mentioned are explicitly identified or placed in italics or quotation marks. They will, nevertheless, be fairly obvious to those who are familiar with the works (for example, extended sections of paraphrased and/or quoted text occur in the first part of poem 5, the second part of poem 25, and the first and third parts of poem 40). Text that is italicised represents either quoted material, or words closely based on quotations from other texts. I gratefully acknowledge my use of all the works referred to above. I would like to thank Shane Strange for his encouragement and publishing expertise and Cassandra Atherton for her very significant editorial contribution. Thanks, too, to Maggie Shapley for her proofreading.

About the author

Paul Hetherington has written and edited more than twenty books and has won or been nominated for numerous national and international prizes. He heads the International Poetry Studies Institute (IPSI) in the Faculty of Arts and Design at the University of Canberra, where he is also Professor of Writing.

2019 Editions
Palace of Memory: An elegy **Paul Hetherington**
Acting Like a Girl **Sandra Renew**
A Coat of Ashes **Jackson**
Summer Haiku **Owen Bullock**
A Common Garment **Anita Patel**
Strange Stars: A queer poetry anthology **Various**
Giant Steps **Various**
Some Sketchy Notes on Matter **Angela Gardner**
The Question Nest **Peter Bakowski**
Breathing in Stormy Seasons **Stephanie Green**
Strange Creatures **Alyson Miller**

2018 Editions
The Uncommon Feast **Eileen Chong**
Inlandia **KA Nelson**
Peripheral Vision **Martin Dolan**
The Love of the Sun **Matt Hetherington**
Moving Targets **Jen Webb**
Things I Have Thought to Tell You Since I Saw You Last **Penelope Layland**
The Many Uses of Mint **Ravi Shankar**
Abstractions **Various**
ACE: Arresting, Contemporary stories by Emerging Writers **Various**

all titles available from

www.recentworkpress.com

www.ingramcontent.com/pod-product-compliance
Lightning Source LLC
Chambersburg PA
CBHW032048290426
44110CB00012B/1009